AWAKE

By
Toccara Ingram

Copyright

ISBN: 979-8-9886335-6-3

For book orders, author's appearances, inquires and interviews, contact: Author Tocarra Ingram engagedti@gmail.com for imprint publishing services contact details@theebonyjbrand.com g

The EbonyJ Brand

Publishing Services

Serves as an umbrella for Publishing, Real Estate, Fashion, and Ministry.

For services

Contact:
details@theebonyjbrand.com

ACKNOWLEDGEMENTS

I want to thank God first and foremost; this journal would not have been possible without a vision, a word, and an instruction to write.

Thank you to my pastors, Melvin and Ashley Cross, at Glory House International. Thank you for your sermons like "Here come the dreamers." I realized that my dreams had meaning; it's the place where I felt something in my belly flowing. It is the place where destiny and purpose were made clear.

Thank you to Prophet Efa Egbe, founder of Bethesda Pools Ministries and The School of the Spirit, as well as the Woman's Academy, for your prayer meetings, activations, and deliverance sessions, which have helped equip and prepare me for my calling.

Thank you to my parents, Jerry and Deborah Ingram, for intentionally guiding me to choose a righteous path, a God ordained path.

Thank you to my siblings and a special shout-out to my sister, Lashawanda Ingram, for being my A1 from day 1. Thanks for supporting me, and being there through thick and thin, and journeying alongside me.

DEDICATION

I dedicate this book to my daughter's, Shadia and Kenya; my sister, Lashawanda; and my niece, Jade.

"Yea, though I walk through the valley of the shadow of death: I will fear no evil, for you are with me; your rod and your staff, they comfort me". (Psalms 23:4)

INTRODUCTION

"Awake" by Toccara Ingram is a journal of prophetic dreams connecting scripture from the Bible, ensuring the dream aligns with divine truth. Scripture (the Word) acts as a foundation to confirm spiritual messages.

It follows one women's spiritual journey with God, who trains and communicates with her using dreams to convey heavenly messages, warnings, and prophecies.

She undergoes three stages: #1 Dreams, which are images, scenes, thoughts, or feelings while asleep; #2 Interpreting dreams, which include analyzing symbols and emotions, and uncovering the meaning of the dream; #3 Becoming the dream, which means you now have to do something to make the dream come to pass.

Just like in the Old Testament, when Joseph (Genesis 37) had a dream of sheaves (bundles of grain) and celestial bodies bowing to him, which angered his brothers, why? Because they were able to interpret the dream. They knew the celestial bodies were symbolic for them, the brothers bowing to him, but to become the dream, Joseph had to be sold into slavery, fulfilling the prophecy later.

In the New Testament, Cornelius (Acts 10), AN angel appears to this Roman centurion in a vision, telling him to send for Peter. A life-changing vision, He took action. Because he obeyed his family, and himself received the good news and salvation.

GOD is the same God of yesterday, today, and forever. He still speaks to us in our dreams. Awake is to make you alert and aware that it's not "just a dream." Pay attention, God is trying to tell you something.

AWAKE

While asleep, I heard these words: "Many are called, but few are chosen." A vision of a book appeared, on the cover, in capital letters, I saw the word 'CHOSEN' with a picture of a bride and groom.

To be chosen means you did not choose it; God chose you out of his mercy and love so that you may know him and love him. To serve as his vessel for a specific purpose or task in his divine plan for his glory. Blessed is she who believes in a vision yet not seen.

"Hath he spoken, shall He not make it good?"

I write in obedience to "ABBA" To convince unbelievers to believe that God's promises are yes, and in him, Amen. To believers, if you doubted, believe again.

Habakkah 2:3, "For the vision is yet for an appointed time, but at the end it shall speak, and not lie: though it tarry, wait for it; because it will surely come, and not lie.

PROPHECY

In the year 2020, I heard God say three words to me twice: "spoken, hurt, and redeemed." It prompted me to ask the Lord what those words meant for me. I heard, "Daughter, it's your testimony."

I give God all the glory; He's the reason I'm telling my story. He heard my heart crying out to him, and he came in and saved me.

Spoken is a prophecy he spoke to me: the three words, a story I'll tell.

It's my testimony of how he saw me through trials and tribulations. When I was hurt, Jesus rushed in and rescued; He paid the ransom for me and you.

BETRAYAL

Late one night, while I was asleep, something in my spirit woke me up. I checked my boyfriend's phone; I'll never forget the words I saw. It read,

"I miss you, my lover, my wife-to-be."

He called her his queen. This was a text to another woman out of the country. I was confused.

How could this be?

After 10 years of being together, he was with me, living together as one big family. I need air; I could not breathe. Something stirred.

As I looked around the living room, I had an epiphany. The walls full of pictures, not one of me. I never saw this coming. It angered me. The memories arose in me: when he would choke me, pin me down, and not let me free. A floor full of screws, screw-ups, and all the things he had done to me. I was blind, but now I could see a clock ticking in front of me.

REJECTION

Depression came sailing in. I was sinking. I met a gentleman who was uplifting.

He gave me validation. He was saying all the right things. He wanted a wife, a baby, a family. He proposed to me. I moved into his home, and we had a baby. I shared with him the things that concerned me. He said,

"This is my house. If you don't like it, you can leave. I can do as I please. I'm a man, do not question me."

He would be nice, then he would be nasty. He would love me, then he would hate me. He would draw close, then he would push me away. If I added all the "he will," it equals double-minded.

A double-minded man is unstable in all his ways (James 1:8).

He was indecisive about being in a relationship with me, marriage, or being a family; He lacked commitment. He refused to change his lifestyle. He would intentionally treat me harshly.

DEPRESSION

I sank into depression. I thought my life was over. I began to have suicidal thoughts, in the form of a question, "Do I want to die? I wasn't sure why I was having this thought. I began to explore the idea, wondering if dying was the key to solving all my problems. I sought the Lord about dying, and He heard me, and He answered. He tells me it is a spirit of depression and teaches me about it.

This spirit had no power over me. *"All authority has been given to me in heaven and on earth." (Mathew 28:18).* The spirit of depression was trying to get me to "agree" to speak death over myself. There is power in the things we speak, so use your words wisely and speak life over death. *Life and death is in the power of our tongue. (Proverbs 18:21)*

One time, as I was driving, I received a nasty text message. It said, "Do you not have family you can go stay with?" I left some boxes in front of the bedroom door, so you can pack your stuff." I thought, I should crash into a wall. The Holy Spirit tells me the enemy was trying to use a thought to get me to "agree" with death. Another time, I got so angry, after he turned off the lights while I was feeding our child. He said "you do not pay the electric bill." The Holy Spirit tells me the enemy was trying to use my emotions to get me to "agree" with death.

HURT

I felt hopeless, lost, and confused. I felt like there was no way out. I had hit rock bottom. Defeated summed up my life. I began desperately crying out to God, anxiously pacing the floor and walking in a circle. That circle represented the shape of my life, with my head held down, staring at the floor.

Ironically, that's how I felt, low, small as dust. Walked over. Trying to make sense of everything. I had been betrayed, and now I'm being rejected. I did not understand why this was happening to me.

I was praying to God to rescue me. I could not go through this again; the betrayal almost killed me. So here I am, Jesus. All I have is a word spoken over my life. Show yourself to be God. When suddenly I heard "look up," a still, small voice said. I was standing in front of an open window. I thought, "God is so strategic while gazing at the big blue sky."

God began to speak. The open window was an invitation to chat: God said, "Look up, need a way out? "God said, 'I AM' the way. Feel like you have nothing? God said, "Let me remind you, you have something." "Who have I created you to be?"

Psalms 34:18 "The Lord is close to the broken-hearted and saves those who are crushed in spirit."

THE GIFT

For years, I have had a recurring dream. I am running with a baby in my arms. It is a girl, and she is tiny. I am not sure what is wrong, but there is a knowing I have to save her.

"For God speaketh once, yet man doth not perceive it. In a dream, in a vision of the night, He opens our ears and sealeth our instructions." (Job 33:14).

I did not take any measures concerning this dream, God gives me another dream with the full picture this time.

I am pregnant. I call out to my father twice, very loudly, "I am about to give birth!" I can feel the baby's head coming out. I lay on the couch and gave birth. It is a girl, and she is tiny.

I learned God was showing me He had given me a gift (baby) to call out to him (Father), and he will help me.

Ephesians 4:7-8 "But to each one of us grace has been given as Christ apportioned it. This is why it says; "when he ascended on high, he took many captives and gave gifts to his people.

RESCUE

I kept seeing 1:11 every time I looked at the clock on the wall or my phone. I would see it on my receipts or on the license plates of cars. I thought, "Why do I keep seeing this number everywhere?" God heard my thoughts; he tells me it's time to leave this toxic relationship; I have spent enough time and do not have any time left to give.

He gives me scripture Ecclesiastes 3:1-11, which starts by saying *"There is a time for everything, and a season for everything under the heavens.."*

Seeing 1:11 was about the time God used the book of Ecclesiastes to show me He's referring to the time and season for me. God begins to build me up by telling me how he sees me. I begin reciting affirmations and scriptures in the mirror every day that God had given me: "I am beautiful," "I am worthy," "I am splendid," "I am above and not beneath," "I am gracefully broken," "I believe I am who God says I am." "I am a child of God."

God said, "It's time to go."

ALIGNMENT

My sister and I are together in her car, she is the driver, and I am the passenger. I am not sure where we are headed. She pulls in front of a huge white house. I do not recognize the house, but I noticed the address is the number 88 in huge red writing, and the street name stood out in bold green letters; it read Delimane. There was a serene feeling that came over me.

In another dream, I am awakened by a knock on the door. My sister says, "It's 11:11; it is time to go."

I was visiting my sister, who lives in a different city, and she took me to see the new house she was going to move into. The house is white, and I thought it looked like the house that was in my dream. But I was not thinking anything else about it. When I went inside, a serene feeling came over me, the same feeling I felt in the dream.

I believed God was telling me to move in with my sister through the dreams. 88 represented new beginning, and "Delimane" means strength. I prayed, and I asked God to confirm that He wanted me to leave my hometown, and He gave me another dream.

I am at bingo, and I yell "bingo" on a straight-line bingo pattern. A way was made when it looked as if my life was over, and so I moved. I learned that the line represented alignment. *Psalms 37:23 "The steps of a good man are ordered by the Lord: and he delighteth in his way."*

EAGLES

I'm driving on my way to my grandma's house. As I'm getting closer to the house, I see birds perched on the roof.

I park. As I approached the house, I noticed they were not just normal birds. They are white eagles. I learned that God was showing me there is a prophetic covering that rest on my maternal grandmother's side. The eagles represented prophetic, and the roof represented a covering. Eagles can also mean and symbolize Majesty and High Vision: They represent high flight, keen vision, and royal power, appearing in prophetic visions (Ezekiel 10:14, Daniel 7:4)

God protects his people like an eagle watching over its young, carrying them on its wings. (Exodus 19:4, Deuteronomy 32:11)

Isaiah 40:31 "But those who hope in the Lord will renew their strength. They will soar on wings like an eagle; they will run and not grow weary, they will walk and not faint."

DAILY BREAD

My father takes three of us to a food pantry, a place where they distribute free food to people in need. There are a lot of people waiting to receive food.

They had given each person bags of food except me; I got handed two loaves of bread. I thought they must expect the three of us to share.

I learned that God was showing me that the Father, the Son, and the Holy Spirit were with me (three people). Take his word (bread) and share it with the people.

Mathew 6:11 " Give us this day our daily bread. There must be a daily dependence on God for all our needs.

Mark 16:15 Jesus says, "Go into the world and preach the gospel to every creature."

John 6:35 "Then Jesus declared, "I am the bread of life. Whoever comes to me will never go hungry, and whoever believes in me will never be thirsty."

ARISE

I am asleep outside, lying flat on my back. I hear someone say, "arise." I begin to rise; It's very windy. I feel the presence of the Holy Spirit flowing through me, and the wind that's coming from all directions. I sit straight up and open my eyes.

Immediately, fright comes over me. Lo and behold, what do I see? An "angel" in front of me. The angel tells me I have something to say.

I learned that to arise means to be stirred up, to be awake, to prepare for action, or to move up to a higher place.

To Abram: "Arise, walk through the land" (Genesis 13:17).

To Joseph (Mary's husband): "Arise, flee into Egypt" (Matthew 2:13)

To Joshua: "Arise, take the people of war, and go up to AI. (Joshua 8:1)

Ezekiel 37:9 "Then he said to me, "Prophesy to the breath; thus says the Lord God: come from the four winds, O breath, into these slain, so that they may live."

DISCERNMENT

I had a powerful experience at Glory House International, a church in Rochester, NY. The Holy Spirit was guiding me to help someone in need.

The first thing that happened was the message Melvin Cross Jr., my pastor, preached; I had heard in a dream the night before service. It's amazing how God can use our dreams for guidance in real life.

While the pastor was preaching, the Holy Spirit began to ask me, "What do you sense?" I said to myself, "depression." The Holy Spirit asked, "Where do you sense it?" I replied, "Upfront near the altar. "The Holy Spirit asked, "What else do you sense?" Through the Holy Spirit, I knew the person was having thoughts of suicide and felt like they had nothing.

The Holy Spirit began to prompt and guide me to go and remind them of their worth, to tell them they are loved and have value, and to remind them who God created them to be. I had never had this type of Holy Spirit encounter.

PROPHESY

"It was Love Sunday; ' church outside the walls.' My team, a team of six of us, was sent to a neighborhood park. Our instructions were to clean the park and minister to someone if you were able to." Two women came into the park and sat on the bench.

The Holy Spirit is nudging me to go speak with them. I thought, "Why me? Surely someone else is more qualified. Besides, I did not want it to rain on anyone's parade. I can see they're getting high.

But the Holy Spirit would not leave me alone. So I say, "God if you want me to go speak, tell me what to say;" I heard, "Tell them that I love them, and I care."

I make my way to them. I ask," Do you mind if I pray really quickly for you guys, then I will get out of your way?" They say yes.

I tell them the Holy Spirit kept nudging me to talk to them, but I did not have anything to say. They both laughed.

I say God sent me over here to tell you He loves you and He cares, I began to pray. The Holy Spirit comes on me, and there is a knowing through the Holy Spirit why God sent me over there.

I began to prophesy to one of the ladies. I tell her that God has been protecting her because He is going to use her. I say I do not know who has been praying for you, but someone has been praying to God for you. I tell her to look around, as the others are cleaning up, that God said He's getting ready to clean her up. As I am prophesying, she is weeping. This is the first time I have prophesied. I learned God is the one who qualifies you.

1Corinthians14:1
"Earnestly desire the spiritual gifts, especially to prophesy.

THE CALL

It is as if I am looking through a set of binocular lenses. I see a man with a gun; he's on a mission. His assignment is to kill. He is on his way to a specific person. They are not aware that he is coming. Some tried to run, even hide, but he knows exactly where they are.

He did not take a break, nor did he rest or sleep; he went from person to person and killed them.

I woke up from this dream, and I asked the Lord, "What did I just watch?" Three times that night, I physically felt an intense pressure – a weight being pressed on me

I learned this was a calling dream. Those people were souls that I'm responsible for; that gunman was a death angel.

Mathew 24:36, "But about that day and hour no one knows."

SUPERNATURAL ENCOUNTER

One morning, I got up and noticed white discharge in my eyes. Throughout the day, my eyes were hurting, so I decided to take a nap. I lay down and closed my eyes. I noticed a light, although I did not think anything of it.

The light began to flash on and off like a flashlight. The light came close to my eyeballs as if I were getting an eye exam. When the light moved away, I realized the light was an angel.

I watched this angel fly higher and higher, past the mountains, through the clouds, into the sky. When it arrived at its destination, it felt as if it took my eyelids and opened them wide, like when you pull back a curtain.

I saw angels flying back and forth. I saw light. I saw fire. I saw an eagle soaring. I saw stars and the universe. I pinched myself just to see if I was awake or not. I learned I had a supernatural encounter.

Psalms 103:20, "Bless the Lord, ye his angels that excel in strength, that do his

commandments, hearkening unto the voice of his word."

GIFT OF TONGUES

It was evening, and I was in my bedroom listening to a sermon on YouTube. The pastor asked if anyone wanted to receive the gift of tongues.

I began to pray with my eyes closed, telling God I desired to receive this gift. A vision of a window appeared; the window turned into a door.

I believed I was about to receive it. My tongue began to flutter very fast, and a language flowed out of my mouth.

I learned the window represented opportunity and the door represented entry.

Acts 2:1-3 "The Holy Spirit descends upon the apostles, and they begin to speak in tongues."

NARROW WAY

I am walking down Rauber Street. I have my daughter, who is riding her power-up electric car with me. The Holy Spirit says, "You can go through the enemy camp or go around." I chose to go through the enemy camp, even though I would have to lift the car over the fence first.

I could see my brother Jerrod sitting on the porch. I thought if I need help to lift it, I'll just call him over.

Rauber here represents a thief. Jerrod means spearman. Spear is the word of God for help. It was going to take strength; hence, I needed to lift the car over a fence and cross over the land. The car represented directions. Or I could have gone around, which would have been easier but took longer. I learned that God was allowing me to pursue the enemy and take back what was stolen.

Matthew 7:13-14 "Enter by the narrow gate; for wide is the gate and broad is the way that leads to destruction, and there are many who go by it. Because narrow is the gate and difficult is the way which leads to life, and there are few who find the way."

TRAINING

The Holy Spirit began to train me using visions and dreams. I would watch a situation among people as if looking through a set of lenses.

When the situation was over, the Holy Spirit would ask me, "What spirit is operating in the person?" Jezebel spirit is a tricky one! The Holy Spirit would correct me and tell me what spirit it was.

I would be shown different spirits, and I would be instructed to rebuke them, or command them to leave in the name of Jesus, or to plead the blood of Jesus.

Ephesians 6:22, "For we are not wrestling against human beings. We are wrestling with rulers, authorities, and spiritual forces that control evil in the heavenly world."

WOLF

I am outside walking on a trail. In the distance, on the other path, a man is walking a dog on a leash. I watched as he walked the dog back and forth in and out of a cave.

As I took a closer look, I could see it was not a dog; it was a wolf. I began to warn the pedestrians not to go that way – there's a wolf over there.

The wolf noticed me and started to charge my way. It is chasing me! I am running as fast as I can. I realized I was on a track, it is a race; I just have to get to the end.

God was showing me that I had a specific task: to warn his people not to go that way. I learned the wolf was a metaphor for danger or destruction.

Acts 20:24 "However, I consider my life worth nothing to me; my only aim is to finish the race and complete the task the Lord Jesus has given me- the task of testifying to the good news of God'

JEZEBEL

I am in my parents' living room. When all of a sudden, Jezebel appears. I call out to my mother, "Help!" but she cannot hear me; I have no voice.

I hear the Holy Spirit say, "You have to fight." The Holy Spirit came upon me and gave me power and might. I pounced on top of her like a lion catching its prey. She is pinned down beneath me. I realized I was stronger; she is weak.

Jezebel promoted worshipping the Canaanite god called Baal, and harassed, oppressed, afflicted, and prosecuted the prophets of Yahweh, the Israelite God.

John 4:4 "Greater is he that is in me, than he that is in this world."

JEZEBEL AND HER GANG

I could sense jezebel and a gang of witches in the vicinity, coming my way. They are at my front door trying to break in.

I thought, since I am outnumbered, that I would sneak out.

I went up to the attic, thinking I would jump down and run out through the backyard. I climb out the window, but a witch is waiting for me. I ran up on her quickly and took her head. I held the head in my hands, looking straight into her eyes, and told her," I am coming for the rest of their heads that were at my front door, too."

I learned there are some battles you cannot avoid; you will have to fight, and you will win. God will give you your Goliath's head.

Ecclesiastes 3: 7-8 "There is a time for war and a time for peace."

JEZEBEL

A stranger, a woman; she shoots an axe at me. It misses me and boomerangs back to her, and she catches it.

She attempts several times. I realize I have a spear in my hand. I throw it, and just like that, it's stuck in her back. She's severely injured. She calls for backup.

I am a soldier; I have to fight, so I put on the full armor of the Lord. I cover myself with the blood of Jesus. I pull my sword using the word of the Lord. Break the arm of the wicked. Beat thy enemy with a medal rod. Beat thy enemy small as dust. Give me the head of my enemy.

I learned to combat challenges by using spiritual weapons, which include putting on the full armor of God, relying on scripture, prayer, fasting, worship, and the blood of Jesus. This is how I fought the battles.

2 Corinthians 10:4 "For the weapons of our warfare are not carnal, but for the pulling down of strongholds."

NO WEAPON FORMED AGAINST ME SHALL PROSPER

I hear gunshots outside. I look out and see the assailant firing at the people from a cloud in the sky.

The assailant notices me helping people get to safety, so he targets me. I get lifted into a cloud in the sky, right in front of the assailant.

I'm shouting, "No weapon formed against me shall prosper," over and over. Bullets are flying all around me.

I learned this particular verse is a promise of God's protection. I can use it for every attempt of harm from the enemy.

Psalms 91:11-12 "For he will command his angels concerning you to guard you in all your ways; they will lift you up in their hands so that you will not strike your foot against a stone."

A WHOLE NEW WORLD

Now I am chilling in my bed when I see a shadow come in. I thought I must be tripping; I imagined it, but there it is again. I thought the Holy Spirit must be training me differently, I guess. Out of nowhere, I feel a stabbing in my head; the smell of weeds and dirt is clogging up my air. Looking around, I see shadows and figures. I'm wondering what all of this is. And then, it hits me what that angel did when it opened up my eyelids. And all the training had been leading up to this. What happened in the spirit first, just hit the earth. I see a whole new world – the Spirit world- and fear took hold of me.

I learned there are two types of eyes: physical eyes, which refer to the literal ability to see the physical world through our senses. Spiritual eyes refer to the ability to perceive spiritual truths and realities beyond the limitations of physical sight.

WOLFS

In the wee hours of the night, I woke up and saw what appeared to be wolves on my ceiling.

There were too many to count. They looked upset. They were growling and snaring.

I was afraid I was vigilant all night until I dozed off, and the Lord gave me a dream. He showed me that I had three angels standing behind me with their bows and arrows drawn.

I learned God was establishing in me a task. Jesus tells his disciples to go! I am sending you out like lambs among wolves. Wolves are individuals who disguise their malicious intentions with a façade of goodness or righteousness.

Matthew 7:15-20 "Watch out for false prophets. They come to you in sheep clothing, but inwardly they are ferocious wolves. By their fruit you will recognize them.

I would watch different prophetic voices on the internet, and later God would show me through a dream how a specific person received their information. I would see a familiar spirit giving the person the information, or they face would be a wolf, or I would see contamination or bubble gum stuck an everything.

1 John 4 ESV says "Beloved do not believe every spirit, but test the spirits to see if they are from God. For many false prophets have gone out into the world.

OVER COMING FEAR

The devil used fear to mentally torment me. I became afraid of the dark. I would see dark figures, shadows, and strange things. I kept my bedroom light on at bedtime, and I would stay awake all night until daylight. The devil would give me nightmares and tell me he was going to kill me. God would give me dreams showing me I had angels protecting me. So, my sister decided we should sleep in the children's room because it had two beds: one for my daughter and the other for my niece, so that we could all bunk together. It did not stop my process, but it gave me some comfort, like when you are walking down a dark alley, and someone is holding your hand.

I would sleep with the cover over my head until the day I had a spiritual attack. I heard the Holy Spirit say, "Take the cover off your head," but I did not listen. Then something tried to smother me. I knew God allowed it. God allowed that attack because He needed me to take the cover from over my head to see the things He wanted to show me and teach me. Another time, I awoke and could not catch my breath. The devil whispered, "Where was your God?" I whispered back, "My God woke me up." I will admit, I prayed for another way; I even thought about asking Him to close my eyes again, but I made it through. Slowly but surely, I learned to just get through the day, which also entailed seeing things. I let tomorrow worry about itself.

Then it occurred to me that when God placed me in a cloud up in the air in front of a gunman, that gunman was satan, the prince of the air. So, I began to annihilate every threat he sent my way. He is already defeated when Jesus shed his blood on Calvary. I went back to my room and slept with the lights off again. And no longer was I afraid to be alone

It took me over a year to conquer fear, but I learned to put my faith, trust, and confidence in God. I learned to stand my ground and take back my power using this word.

"No weapon formed against me shall prosper," **Isaiah 54:27.**

OPEN DOOR

I'm in the house, lying underneath a blanket in the living room on the floor. The front door is open. I see a black bird sitting on the power line outside; it has two heads and a domino piece on its neck. It was a warning dream. God was showing me the enemy planned to attack and cause a domino effect. God was also showing me that He was covering me; I'm underneath a blanket.

The open door that gave the enemy power (hence it's on a power line) was unforgiveness. I learned through a vision. God showed me a person's face, and I heard the word "unforgiveness." I quickly forgave and closed the door.

Ephesians 4:47 "And do not give the devil an opportunity to lead you into sin by holding a grudge, or nurturing anger, or harboring resentment, or cultivating bitterness."

THE ADVERSARY

I had worshiped all day long into the night. Out of nowhere, strange light flashes appeared in my room.

At first, I thought of angels. Suddenly, that light figure turned into a lion. I continue to worship as I keep my eye on it.

It would arch its back and blow. I could feel cold air each time it blew. It seemed as if it was trying to blow out a fire. I learned by feeding myself with the word of God, praying, fasting, and worshipping, and I had developed a spiritual fire.

1 Peter 5:8 "Be sober, be vigilant; because your adversary the devil goes about like a roaring lion, seeking whom he can devour."

MY ANGEL

I noticed a being that looked human formed on my wall. Every room I went into, it would be there.

I can sense it was watching over me; I felt peace, and I felt safe. I ask the Lord, "What is that?" and he gave me a dream.

It is as if I am looking through binoculars; I see a portrait on a wall- it's the being I saw on my walls. I see a name, and it also says "Angel." Then the angel waves to me and turns back to a portrait.

Psalms 34:7-8 " The angel of the Lord encampeth round about them that fear him and delivereth them. In taste and see that the Lord is good: blessed is the man that trusteth in him."

DELIVERANCE

They say I am acting different. "Yup," people are judging me. I cannot imagine the hurt Jesus felt trying to convince unbelievers to believe.

Can I tell you what the Lord did for me? There was a situation back home; he turned it around for me.

On hard days when I felt like giving up, he blew the breath of life into my body, so I could live, not sleep.

He dropped down a rose from heaven just to show me he cares. And when I called on his name, "Jesus," He walked with me. He talked with me.

He let the power of his presence fall down heavenly on me; demons had to flee.

Deliverance even happened while I was asleep; pastors would lay their hands on my head, and Jesus would set me free.

He saved my life. "Yup," the glory goes to G-O-D; He parted the Sea, so I can walk free.

"Therefore, if the son makes you free, you shall be free indeed"(John 8:36)

I learned God was calling me to the ministry of deliverance through my dreams. I would see myself placing my hands or throwing anointing oil on someone, commanding demons to come out, using the name of Jesus.

Luke 11:20 " But if I cast out demons with the finger of God, surely the kingdom of God has come upon you."

INTERCESSORY PRAYER

Intercessory prayer is the act of praying to God on behalf of someone else. God would show me in a dream what to pray for. Sometimes it would be to cover them with the blood of Jesus, or for deliverance, or to not fall in a trap or caught in a snare, or for mercy.

One time, I was interceding for someone, after God showed me in a dream that the person had been shot and killed. The enemy gave me a dream, where demons were telling me to let them have the person. God gave me a dream right after, and the person is saying, "Thank you for praying for me." Guess what? The person did get shot, on two different occasions, but through prayer, they did not die. The glory goes to God. Another time, I tarried all night long into the a.m. in prayer on behalf of someone, asking God to have mercy on them. Finally, I heard in my spirit, " Hallelujah, you have won the victory."

I learned prayer is essential; prayer is key; prayer can change everything. " The effectual fervent prayer of a righteous man availeth much," James 5:16

THIEF

"I got it, I caught the thief." Something strange would happen at nighttime. I would see a spider, or its web. I learned through the holy spirit that these signs were an indication of someone practicing witchcraft.

This had been happening for some time, but on this particular night, I could feel it was close behind me. So I decided to check it out.

I turned around and was startled by what I saw. I saw a sly grin on a familiar face- the person the enemy had been secretly using to steal from me in the middle of the web.

The enemy's plans backfired; the same trap they had set for me is the same trap they fell into.

Proverbs 6:31 " But when he is caught, he must pay back seven times what he stole."

MY RESPONSE TO GOD

Here I am, Lord, signed, sealed, delivered, I'm yours. I want you, Lord and only you, and everything you have for me. I chose you, Lord.

I say "Yes to your will, Yes to your way, Yes to your pre-ordained plans for my life, Yes to the assignment. *"May your will be done on earth as it is in heaven (Mathew 6:10).*

Thank you, Lord, for preserving my baby(gift). She still has to be nourished, fed, and grow. I still need prophetic training and a mentor. My prayer is: take my hand, Lord, and lead me to the road. Show me what path to take, and I'll go.

It's time to make a change; we are the people who can do it.

I'm stronger, I'm wiser, I'm better. All that's left to say is hallelujah.

AGAPE LOVE

So I've been in love a time or two, but no one loves like God~ a love that is pure and true love is patient, love is kind. It does not envy, it does not boast, it is not proud, it is not rude, it is not self-seeking, it is not easily angered, it keeps no record of wrong, love does not delight in evil but rejoices with truth.

Agape is God born into sin so that I may live again. What a merciful God.

You did what no man could. You gave me a second chance.

That's why I worship you with my hands, shout, and dance. You deserve the honor and the praise. Worthy is your name.

REDEEMED

Allow me to reintroduce myself. My name is Toccara Ann Ingram, and I am a seer, called to the ministry of deliverance.

"Many are the plans in a person's heart, but it is the Lord's purpose that prevails."- Proverbs 19:21

My problems had me bound; depression weighed me down. That cunning devil planted a seed~ the thought of dying he presented to me- But God kept me.

The Lord made a way of escape for me when there was no way. Jesus is the only way, the truth, and the light. No one will enter to the Father unless they come through Him.

When my enemies tried to triumph, they could not. If God be for me, who can be against me?

God revealed himself in many ways depending on my situation. When I needed help, He gave me a hand. He showed up as Elohim, God my helper.

When I cried out to him, He inclined his ear. He showed up as Abba, God my father.

When I was being treated harshly, he checked up on me. He showed up as El Roi, the God who sees.

When I thought there was no way out, he directed me. He showed up as Jehovah Raah, the Lord my Shepherd.

When I thought I had nothing, He promised I would never beg for bread. He showed up as Jehovah Jirah, the Lord my Provider.

When I was being mentally tormented, He gave me a gift. He showed up as Saar Shalom, Prince of Peace.

When arrows and bullets were being shot at me, He raised his banner. He showed up as Jehovah Gibbor, the Lord mighty in battle.

When He spoke, He showed up as Jesus Christ. This name means "The Anointed One," the one who saves. It is the name above all names. At the name of Jesus, demons flee. He is the bridegroom, and we are his bride. When he returns, every knee will bow in heaven and on earth and profess He is Lord and Savior, the God who Redeems.

www.ingramcontent.com/pod-product-compliance
Lightning Source LLC
Chambersburg PA
CBHW070014100426
42741CB00012B/3235